SCIENCE & TECHNOLOGY

KU-638-261

INTERNET

SCIENCE & TECHNOLOGY

INTERNET

Mason Crest

Mason Crest

Mason Crest

450 Parkway Drive, Suite D
Broomall, PA 19008
www.masoncrest.com

Printed and bound in the United States of America.

Series ISBN: 978-1-4222-4205-6
Hardback ISBN: 978-1-4222-4210-0
EBook ISBN: 978-1-4222-7603-7

First printing
1 3 5 7 9 8 6 4 2

Cover photograph by Anton Balazh/Shutterstock.

Library of Congress Cataloging-in-Publication Data
Names: Mason Crest Publishers, author. Title: Internet / by Mason Crest. Other titles: Internet (Mason Crest Publishers)
Description: Broomall, PA : Mason Crest, [2019] | Series: Science & technology
Identifiers: LCCN 2018034419| ISBN 9781422242100 (hardback) | ISBN 9781422242056 (series) | ISBN 9781422276037 (ebook)
Subjects: LCSH: Internet--Juvenile literature.
Classification: LCC TK5105.875.I57 I53475 2019 | DDC 004.67/8--dc23 LC record available at https://lccn.loc.gov/2018034419

QR Codes disclaimer:

CONTENTS

KEY ICONS TO LOOK FOR

Words to Understand: These words with their easy-to-understand definitions will increase the reader's understanding of the text, while building vocabulary skills.

Sidebars: This boxed material within the main text allows readers to build knowledge, gain insights, explore possibilities, and broaden their perspectives by weaving together additional information to provide realistic and holistic perspectives.

Educational Videos: Readers can view videos by scanning our QR codes, providing them with additional educational content to supplement the text. Examples include news coverage, moments in history, speeches, iconic moments, and much more!

Text-Dependent Questions: These questions send the reader back to the text for more careful attention to the evidence presented here.

Research Projects: Readers are pointed toward areas of further inquiry connected to each chapter. Suggestions are provided for projects that encourage deeper research and analysis.

Series Glossary of Key Terms: This back-of-the-book glossary contains terminology used throughout this series. Words found here increase the reader's ability to read and comprehend higher-level books and articles in this field.

WORDS TO UNDERSTAND

accessible to be approachable or easily contacted

advantage something that is beneficial

advantage benefit or gain

ajax a web development technique used for creating interactive web applications

amateur someone who does something for pleasure rather than for professional reasons or money

amaze to surprise

comparatively in comparison

convert to change

destination address

display reveal or show

employment work or occupation

encourage to motivate or inspire

enhance to make greater or improve the quality

giant huge

humor something that is laughable or funny

icon image, figure, or representation displayed on a computer screen

immediately at once

incorporate make into a whole or make part of a whole

independent free from any kind of control

innovative to do new things; to think differently from others

interactive providing output based on input from the user

interconnected connected with each other

invent to find new things or to devise something new

library a collection of literary documents or records kept for reference or borrowing

logical thinking critical thinking involved in determining the meaning and significance of what is observed or expressed

modem equipment used in computers to communicate with other computers

notable important or famous

oddity something strange or unusual

pandemic a disease that is spread throughout the world

polylines a term for a line used by some geographic information systems (GIS) packages

primary content important content

protocol a set of rules that is used by computers to communicate with each other across a network

resolution the number of pixels per square inch on a computer-generated display

satellite an automatic moving object in space that captures pictures and sends signals for radio and TV

scan to examine something closely in order to look for a particular thing

surf the activity of looking for various things one after another at the same time on the Internet or the world wide web

technology the practical application of science to commerce or industry

urban related to towns or cities

web link a reference to a document that the reader can directly follow, or that is followed automatically

History of the Internet

The history of the Internet began in the late 1960s. The idea of joining computers first came into the mind of J. C. R. Licklider of Massachusetts Institute of **Technology** (MIT) in 1962.

INTRODUCTION

The Internet is a means of connecting one computer to another anywhere on the globe. It is called the network of networks, spread all over the world like a web. When two or more computers are interconnected with each other, they can easily send or receive any kind of information, such as text, voice, videos, and so on. The Internet allows us to download or upload information, send or receive emails, watch videos, chat online, play games, etc. With the help of the Internet, we can visit websites that help us in getting knowledge of different things. It has become an easily accessible channel for information and entertainment.

First Use of the Internet

The first person to use the Internet was Charley Kline, a University of California, Los Angeles, student programmer. He transmitted the first message over the ARPANET on October 29, 1969. He had to send the message text "LOGIN." He successfully typed the letters L and O of the word "LOGIN," but after that, the system crashed. An hour later, after recovering from the crash, the SDS Sigma 7 computer accepted the full "LOGIN."

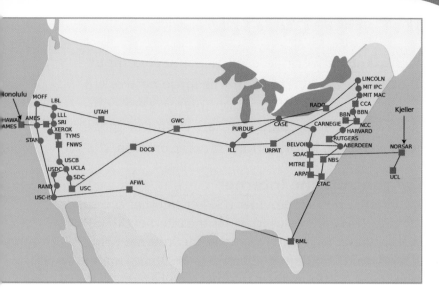

ARPANET

The head of the US Defense Advanced Research Projects Agency, Robert Taylor, with Larry Roberts from MIT started working on Licklider's idea. After hard work, they connected two computers successfully between the University of California, Los Angeles, and the Stanford Research Institute on October 29, 1969. This network was called ARPANET. The ARPANET developed rapidly and more than two hundred computers were connected by 1981.

SCIENCE FACTS

- Today, about a dozen countries lack regular Internet connections. The "unconnected" are mostly blocked by their governments.

- Donald Davies **invented** the concept of "packet switching" at the UK National Physical Laboratory in the early 1960s.

Internet

A number of various **independent** networks like CSNET, BITNET, and JANET were created in the US and United Kingdom until the early 1980s. By 1987, a large number of independent networks joined and formed a huge network called the INTERNET.

A Giant Network

The Internet, a **giant** network, is used to connect computers from all over the world. Through this large network, a computer can send or receive information to any other computer. The Internet connects computers all over the globe with each other to ease the information-transfer process.

ISP controls the Internet

An Internet service provider (ISP) or Internet access provider (IAP) allows us to access the Internet. An ISP is a company that connects us to the Internet using a **modem**, DSL (digital subscriber line), dial-up, or other means. ISP provides Internet email accounts to us so that we can communicate, sending or receiving information to relatives and friends in different parts of the world. Today, a number of ISPs have developed. ISPs have servers that assist them in controlling the Internet.

Working of the Internet

The working of the Internet is similar to that of the post office. When we send a letter through post office, we have to write the origin and **destination** address on it. Similarly, when we send information via the Internet, we have to write the origin and destination address on it so that the other end can easily receive the information. In the post office, a postal worker delivers or receives the information. Likewise, in the case of the Internet, wires and **satellites** work as postal workers through which we can send or receive information. The Internet sends or receives information in small packages.

SCIENCE FACTS

- China has the highest number of Internet users.

- There are a large number of ISPs around the world. They are interconnected at Internet exchange points (IXs) that allow the passage of information among them.

Connecting Your Computer to the Internet

Today, a large number of means are available to connect your computer to the Internet. You can easily access the Internet by using various ways depending on the location of your computer.

Satellite

Satellite broadband services are an efficient way to access the Internet. This provides Internet access at a very high speed to any location and even while on the move. Low earth orbit (LEO) satellites are used to provide Internet access.

Dial-up

Dial-up method is the slowest way to connect to the Internet. It provides connection through existing phone lines. It can be available at any location, if you have a landline telephone.

DSL

Digital subscriber line (DSL) connects computers to the Internet through the wires of a local telephone network. DSL provides high frequency access to the Internet through an existing telephone line.

Cable Modem

Cable modem is the best as well as cheapest option to connect the Internet with your computer. This network bridge provides communication between two computers. It is used to provide high-speed Internet access via television cables.

SCIENCE FACTS

- The measurement unit of a modem is bits per second (bit/s or bps).
- DSL originally was the abbreviation for digital subscriber loop.

World Wide Web

The World Wide Web, abbreviated as WWW, is one of the services offered by the Internet. The WWW is a vast informational network. It is a collection of various interconnected documents, sites, and other resources. These resources further contain text, graphics, sound, etc., that provide us with knowledge and information about various things.

Why is it called a Web?

It is called World Wide Web because it is a web of information. Like the silken threads of a spider's web, the information on the Web is interconnected with each other. Thus, you can easily go from one resource of information to another with a single click on its link.

Differences Between the Internet and the Web

There is a huge difference between the Internet and the Web. The Internet is a network of computers, whereas the Web is a network of information. The Internet is used to connect the millions of computers worldwide. On the other hand, the Web is a method of accessing information through the Internet.

SCIENCE FACTS

- Sir Tim Berners-Lee invented the World Wide Web in 1990.

- The domain names of most websites on the internet begin with www. This is a reference to the service that is being sought.

Web Browsers and Search Engines

A web browser is a software program installed on computers that helps in accessing the Internet. The purpose of a web browser is to connect us to the Internet and search engines that further aid us in getting information. Internet Explorer, Mozilla Firefox, Safari, and Google Chrome are some **notable** web browsers.

Searching the Web

The most useful application of the Internet is to search for information. You can easily search anything by just typing the phrase or keyword you want to learn about in any search engine. As soon as you type the word in the search engine, like a spider it starts crawling the World Wide Web, searching for that word. Afterward, the search engine shows numerous information resources on the screen that contain the word that you typed.

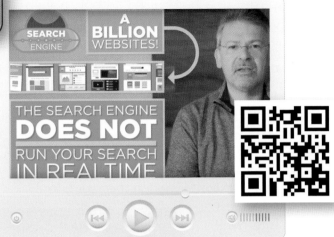

How do search engines work?

Search Engines

A web search engine is a software program that aids in accessing the information on the World Wide Web. With the help of search engines, we can search any information that may consist of pages, images, videos, and so on. Google, Yahoo, and Bing are the most popular search engines.

SCIENCE FACTS

- Mosaic is the first graphical Web browser developed in 1993.

- People around the world make about 3.5 billion Google searches each day.

Websites

A website can be compared to a book. Like a book, a website also contains pages that are called web pages. As the pages of a book contain information, a website is also a collection of information that may include articles, text, graphics, etc. A website can be developed by an individual, a company, or an organization.

Types of Websites

Today, the Internet is loaded with millions of websites. Websites can be of different types according to the information they contain.

- Commercial websites are the most common website on the Internet, used for selling and buying products & services.
- Personal websites provide information about an individual.
- Organizational websites are made to promote the views of a group.
- Educational websites are dedicated to providing information to students about various educational establishments.
- Entertainment websites are designed to entertain users through music, games, etc.
- News websites provide information about current events.
- Blogs are websites that act as a personal diary, maintained by individuals. They may contain an article, opinion, personal information, and so on.

Website Address

There are millions of people alive on the earth. If you want to find your friend among a huge crowd, you will find him through his unique identity or address. Likewise, a large number of websites are present on the Internet. Thus, every website has its unique identity, or address, so that we can find it easily. The unique identity or address of a website is called the uniform resource locator (URL), which was invented by Tim Berners-Lee, Marc Andreessen, Mark P. McCahill, Alan Emtage, Peter J. Deutsch, and Jon Postel in 1994. As soon as we type a URL in a web browser, it starts searching for that URL on the Internet. Within nanoseconds, the desired website opens up on the browser window.

Favorites and Bookmarks

While searching on the Internet, we come across various websites containing text, images, graphics, videos, and so on. Sometimes, we like them and want to keep them with us forever. To keep the website with us and keep a track of it, we have the Favorites and Bookmarks option.

Accessing Your Favorite Web Page

You can see your favorite web page anytime. Whenever you want to see your favorite web page, added in the list of Favorites and Bookmarks, you just have to click the Favorites and Bookmarks icon on the main toolbar. When you click the Favorites and Bookmarks icon, there will be a drop-down menu. In the drop-down menu, you will find a list containing your favorite pages. From the list, you can click the web page and see it.

Adding a Web Page to Favorites and Bookmarks

It is easy to add your favorite web page to the list of Favorites and Bookmarks. The Favorites and Bookmarks icons can be easily seen on the menu bar of web browsers. First, click on the Favorites and Bookmarks icon, then choose "add to Favorites and Bookmarks." After clicking that, the web page will be added to your Favorites and Bookmarks list.

SCIENCE FACTS

- Bookmarks were first **incorporated** in the Mosaic browser with the name "Hotlists."

- "Favorites" is an **icon** present in the web browser Internet Explorer, whereas "Bookmarks" is available on Mozilla Firefox, Safari, Google Chrome, and so on.

Email

An electronic mail, known as email, is like an electronic letter. We write a message in a letter and send it via the post office. Likewise, in the world of the Internet, we write a message in an email and send it through the Internet. Once you log in to an email account, you can easily send or receive emails.

Receiving or Sending an Email

You can send or receive emails via your email address. An email address is like the postal address. It is your unique identity, to which people will send you an email. An email message is comprised of two parts. One is the message header, including the sender, the receiver email address, and the subject of the email The other is the body, including the message. You can check received emails in the "Inbox" section, and send emails via the "Compose mail" option.

- Raymond Samuel Tomlinson was the first one to use an email system in 1971 on the ARPANET.

- The typographic character @, stands for "located at," and is added as a prefix to service providers (@yahoo.com, @gmail.com, etc.) in your email address.

Generating an Email Account

Creating an email account is simple. Various email service providers like Yahoo, Gmail, and others, are available on the Internet. First, choose an email service provider, and then visit its mail web page. There, click on the "Sign up" option. After that, you will get a form including such details as your name, address, username, etc. After filling out the form and agreeing to the terms and conditions, your email account will be ready to use.

Chat and Message

Online chatting and messaging is the most popular means of communication through the Internet. It allows you to stay in touch with your friends, relatives, etc. As soon as you type something on your screen and press enter, the message is **displayed** on the screen of your friend or relative, or whomever you are chatting with. You can chat with multiple users at the same time.

Chatting and Messaging Service Providers

Online chatting and messaging is the simplest way to keep in touch with anyone in real time. You can chat and message through programs like AOL Instant Messenger (AIM), Google Talk, Yahoo! Messenger, Talker, etc., available on the Internet. You can also send **web links**, videos, images, sounds, files, etc., through chat.

- Internet chatting was developed in 1988 by Jarkko Oikarinen.

- The Bitnet Relay, operated on the BITNET, inspired the chat system.

Using Chatting and Messaging

You can start chatting and messaging with your friends and relatives by just downloading any chatting and messaging service provider. After downloading the software, create your account clicking the "sign up" option. When your account is created successfully, you must click into the chat room. In the chat room, a number of individuals are available, who are online at that time. From the list, find your friend's name and click on it. After clicking, a small window will appear on your screen. Just type your message into the box and press "enter" and the message will appear on your friend's computer screen.

Viruses

An Internet virus is a program that can severely infect your computer. A virus can easily multiply itself and spread from one computer to another. It can enter into your computer via email, files, floppy disk, CD, DVD, USB drive, etc. After entering into a computer, a virus can harm its data and performance.

Dangers of Viruses

A virus is a destructive man-made program. It spreads like a communicable disease from one computer to another through various ways. When a virus enters a computer, it stores itself in the computer memory. From there, it starts creating copies of itself. Whenever, you save any data in the computer memory, you also save the virus. It also copies itself from one program to another when you open programs one by one without shutting down the computer. Gradually, it multiplies and infects the whole computer.

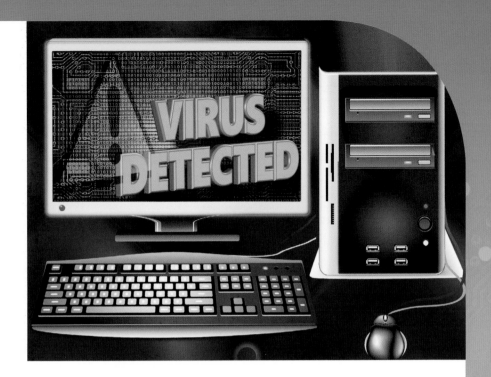

Antivirus

Antivirus software is used to detect, prevent, and remove viruses from the computer. Avast Free Antivirus, AVG Antivirus, McAfee VirusScan, and Norman Antivirus, are just some of the examples of antivirus software. It is like a security guard that saves a computer from any kind of harm done by viruses. As soon as any file or program is download-ed on a computer, the antivirus starts **scanning** it for viruses. If it detects a virus, it removes the virus immediately. Some antivirus software are free to download, whereas some must be bought.

SCIENCE FACTS

- The term "virus" was first used in 1972 in a science fiction novel, *When Harlie was One*, by David Gerrold.

- In 1987, Bernd Fix performed the first publicly docu-mented removal of a computer virus in the wild.

Using the Internet Safely

The Internet is an amazing world of information. It **enhances** your knowledge and skills. But you should use the Internet safely while you are searching for something, chatting, or sending and receiving mail. Using the Internet carelessly may harm you and your computer as well.

Safe Surfing

Surf safe, be safe. If you keep some points in mind while surfing, you can protect yourself as well as your computer. Always follow the rules set by your Internet service provider. Always beware of the virus. Keep in mind that viruses can enter your computer and harm it. Do not click on threatening, abusive, or any other kind of link that makes you feel uncomfortable.

Chat Room and Email Caution

When you are in a chat room or checking your emails, you should keep some points in mind. Never reveal your personal information in the chat. Always keep your password to yourself. Do not tell anyone your password. Never give your email addresses to people you do not know, nor click on strange emails. Never talk on the phone or arrange face-to-face meetings with anyone you meet online without telling your parents.

Uploading and Downloading

Uploading and downloading information, whether a file, photos, music, games, videos, etc., is a popular application of the Internet. Uploading and downloading data has become a common practice and popular activity. Millions of users upload and download files every day.

Uploading

Uploading information means sending data from one computer to another. The data can be a file, photo, music, game, or video. In other words, uploading means loading information from your computer to other resources. You can easily upload anything to a web server, File Transfer Protocol (FTP) server, email server, and so on. You can also upload any data to a website, but only after getting permission from the website owner.

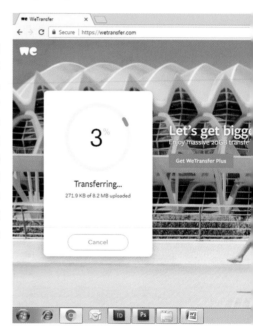

SCIENCE FACTS

- File compression software can be used to turn large files, such as videos, into smaller files suitable for uploading.

- In November 2006, Google Inc. bought YouTube, LLC for $1.65 billion.

Downloading

In the computer world, when you receive any information like a file, software, music, or video to your computer from any remote system, it is called downloading. In other words, downloading means you are loading something in your computer from another resource. You can download a file, video, movie, and so on from the web server or email server. The download time of any data depends on its size. If you download a movie, it will take hours to download, whereas if you download a file, it will take **comparatively** less time.

File transfer basics

Internet and Education

The Internet is a pool of information. With the help of the Internet, you can search, work, play, enhance your knowledge, and complete your homework. Online dictionaries, libraries, educational websites, articles, blogs, and so on, are loaded on the Internet to help you in your studies. The Internet gives you ample resources that provide enough information on various topics.

Make Your Homework Interesting

Homework is boring for many students. But you can make it interesting by seeking the help of the Internet. Various educationa websites are available on the Internet that help you enhance you knowledge and give you lots of matter to complete your home work. The technology and digital objects on the Internet increas your interest and turn the boredom of your homework into fur Many experts give answers to questions posed by the student Various articles are available on the Internet to teach you how t solve problems and find answers to questions.

Interactive Learning

The Internet helps in enhancing your reading, writing, and arithmetic skills in an **interactive** manner. You can develop new skills and improve your **logical thinking** with the help of the Internet. Through the Internet, you can learn new things by watching digital objects and reading about them in detail with numerous resources. Today, the Internet has access to every major **library** in the world, such as the Oxford University Library, Library of Congress, and others, which aid you in finding books.

SCIENCE FACTS

- The online learning market grows about 100 percent each year.

- About 50 percent of students send emails to their teachers to express views that they would not have shared in class.

Social Networking

Social Networking is a way to connect with your friends, relatives, etc. It is a grouping of people to share their ideas, experiences, interests, and so on. Today, social networking is done to meet other people, gain knowledge, find **employment**, enhance business, and so on.

Social Networking Websites

Social networking websites, commonly known as social sites, are websites that allow individuals to create a social network. Facebook and Twitter are examples of social networking websites. You can easily create an account on social networking websites by filling out a simple form at no cost. After creating an account, you can stay in touch with your friends, relatives, and others, anywhere in the world. In some social networking websites, options for chatting, sharing photos and videos, writing blogs, playing games and more, are also available.

ocial Networking and Education

ocial networking plays a major role in education. Through social etworking, you can talk about your studies with your friends, hare your problems with them, and get your problem solved. oday, social networking is being used to improve relationships etween teachers and students as well. You can talk about any aatter with your teacher through social networking, if you are esitant to share the problem in class.

SCIENCE FACTS

- According to the National School Boards Association, almost 60 percent of students use social networking to talk about education.

- Every day, more than 1.5 million web links, blog posts, news stories, notes, etc., are shared on Facebook.

Online Games

Online games can be played on the Internet, using an Internet browser. Most of the online games are free and can be played for an unlimited time. A large number of online games ranging from simple texts to complex graphics are available on the Internet. Some online multiplayer games such as Final Fantasy XI, World of Warcraft, and Lineage II are paid games, whereas some like RuneScape or Tibia are free to play.

Browser Games

Browser games are those games that are played on web browsers. Different browser games are available on the Internet, from single player to multiplayer. Some browser games are also known by the technologies used in them like "Flash games" or "Java games". Browser-based pet games are the most popular games among youths. Recently developed browser games are designed using web technologies like **Ajax** to enable complicated multiplayer games.

History

The history of online games reaches back to the year 1990. During the 1990s, online games moved from local area network (LAN) protocols to the Internet. Doom, a first person shooter video game, became popular as an **innovative** online game. After Doom was introduced, various first-person shooter games started coming online. By the late 1990s, with the development of the Internet, real-time strategy (RTS) games allowed players from different parts of the globe to play with each other. Over time, various home video game consoles, such as the Sega Dreamcast, Sony PlayStation 2, Nintendo GameCube, and Microsoft Xbox entered online gaming on the Internet.

Online Libraries

Online libraries are libraries available on the Internet. Online libraries provide access to online collections of books that can be read through the Internet. With the help of an online library, we can find any book on any topic and read it from home or school. Like a real world library, an online library is also divided into various sections based on topics that help you in finding your choice of book.

History

The term *digital library* was used in print for the first time in a report to the Corporation for National Research Initiatives in 1988. In 1994, the term was popularized by the NSF/DARPA/NASA Digital Libraries Initiative. Project Gutenberg, also known as PG, is the oldest digital library, and **encourages** the creation of ebooks. Over time, a large number of digital libraries have been opened. Google Book Search, Cornell University, Internet Archive, and the Library of Congress's World Digital Library are some of the examples of best online libraries.

Advantages of Online Libraries

The prime **advantage** of the online library is that it provides 24-hour online access to the visitors. Besides providing access to online books, online libraries also offer digitized audio and video. You can easily search any kind of article, materials, notes, etc., by using online libraries. You can use online libraries from any location, as you do not have to go somewhere physically. You can keep the online books to yourself forever after downloading them from the online library.

The Library of Congress online

Google Maps

Google Maps are maps on Google with which you can easily locate any nook and corner of the globe. It **amazes** you with its ability to help you learn the world's geographical boundaries. It provides you with street maps, **urban** business locators, route planners, and so on.

History

Google Maps was developed by Lars and Jens Rasmussen for the company "Where 2 Technologies." In October 2004, Where 2 Technologies was acquired by Google Inc., and **converted** into a web application known as Google Maps. On February 8, 2005, the application was first published on the Google Blog and then at Google.

More on Google Maps

Google Moon is a feature of Google Maps, and shows satellite images of the moon. You can see the planet Mars with Google Mars. Google Sky allows you to see a map of the universe. Through Google My Maps, you can make your own map using markers, **polylines**, and polygons. Google Flu Shot Finder, available in the United States, helps people to locate areas where **pandemic** H1N1/09 viruses and seasonal flu vaccines are available.

Have Fun with Google Maps!

With Google Maps, you can see high-**resolution** satellite images of urban areas in the United States, Canada, the United Kingdom, Australia and many other countries. Most of the satellite images are taken from aircraft. With the zoom in or zoom out option, you can set the resolution as you wish. With Google Maps, you can also get directions that help you find routes in real time. With this option, you have to key in the origin and destination points and Google Maps will give you all the routes.

Videos

Online videos are short clips of long videos that can be watched on the Internet. As the Internet developed, video clips on the Internet also became very popular. By mid-2006, tens of millions of video clips were available online. Online video clips can be developed and uploaded on the Internet by an individual, community, organization, media resource, and so on. Shockinghumor, YouTube, Google Video, MSN Video, and Yahoo! Video are some examples of online video websites.

Types of Online Videos

Online videos often show moments of **humor**, **oddity**, performance, and other similar content. Online videos may be of different types depending on the application. They can show an advertisement or deliver any message. Some video clips are developed by **amateurs**, who can show their talent to the world. A video blog, or vlog, is a type of blog that contains video as its **primary content**. Some online videos are short clips of movies. News clips and popular television content can also be viewed on the Internet.

Webcam

A webcam is a video camera that is easily hooked to a computer and to the Internet. It allows videos or images to be **immediately** transmitted to the server so that they can be accessed by other computers. With a webcam, you can easily do video conferencing with friends and relatives in any part of the world.

TEXT-DEPENDENT QUESTIONS

1. Describe how the ARPANET became the Internet.

2. What does ISP stand for?

3. Who is Sir Tim Berners-Lee?

4. What does the text say was the first graphical Web browser?

5. What does HTML stand for?

6. How does a virus harm computers? What software can combat them?

7. Name three online gaming platforms mentioned in the text.

8. Name one of the interesting ways Google Maps goes beyond the Earth.

RESEARCH PROJECTS

1. The issue of connection speed is a huge topic on the Internet. Look into how fast your computer connects compared to how fast other countries' speeds are. Research ways you can improve your speed. What services or devices are available? And find out why connection speed matters so much!

2. Though it might seem that "everyone" is connected to the Internet, that is not the case. Billions of people around the world, and millions in the United States, do not have regular access to the Web. Find out why this is so and do a chart of ways that governments, nonprofits, and companies are trying to make access more fair.

3. Try this personal experiment: For a day, write down how many times you use the Internet, whether that is for school, work, social networking, or other uses. Then see if you can go a whole day without doing ANY of those things. What was the experience like? Do you think dependence on the Internet is a good thing or a troubling thing? Perhaps organize a discussion group among your friends on this topic.

FIND OUT MORE

Books

Brezina, Corona. *Careers in Digital Media*. New York: Rosen Young Adults Publishing, 2018.

Steffens, Jeffrey. *How the Internet Is Changing the World*. San Diego: Reference Point Press, 2018.

Turing, John Dermot. *The Story of Computing*. London, UK: Arcturus, 2018.

On the Internet

Future of the Internet
http://www.nethistory.info/History%20of%20the%20Internet/future.html
This article is the conclusion of a long site focusing on the development and history of the Internet.

Khan Academy Internet Basics
https://www.khanacademy.org/partner-content/code-org/internet-works
A popular education site offers into on Internet basics.

Inside Google
https://www.google.com/search/howsearchworks/
Find out how all those Google searches work!

alloy a substance made up of a mixture of metals

capacitor a device that stores electricity

emission the act of sending out gases or heat into the atmosphere

digital expressed as series of the digits 0 and 1

friction a force that is produced when one object rubs against another object

hydraulic using powered created by water or liquid

interactive providing output based on input from the user

interplanetary a space mission that is planned for study of other planets

magnetic field a region around a magnet that has the ability to attract other magnets

microprocessor a very small circuit used in computers that performs all the functions of a central processing unit (CPU)

navigation the science of directing the course of a vehicle

programmable able to be given instructions to do a task

protocol a set of rules that is used by computers to communicate with each other across a network

renewable something that can replace itself by a natural process

rechargeable something that can be charged again and again

sensor a mechanical device that is sensitive to some signal and helps in responding to it

voltage difference in electric tension between two points

synchronize to operate two or more devices at the same time

viable capable of working successfully

INDEX

Photo Credits